D0463340

Valentine's Day is a winter celebration

Valentine's Day

Steve Potts

A+

Smart Apple Media

COPYRIGHT

Published by Smart Apple Media

1980 Lookout Drive, North Mankato, MN 56003

Designed by Rita Marshall

Copyright © 2002 Smart Apple Media. International copyright reserved in all countries. No part of this book may be reproduced in any form without written permission from the publisher.

Printed in the United States of America

Photographs by Archive Photos, Bruce Carr, Keystone Press, Paul McMahon, Richard Nowitz, Bonnie Sue Rauch

Library of Congress Cataloging-in-Publication Data

Potts, Steve. Valentine's Day / by Steve Potts. p. cm. – (Holidays series)

Includes bibliographical references and index.

ISBN 1-58340-119-9   1|21|02

1. Valentine's Day–Juvenile literature. [1. Valentine's Day. 2. Holidays.] I. Title.

GT4925 .P68 2001   394.2618–dc21   00-067712

First Edition 9 8 7 6 5 4 3 2 1

Valentine's Day

CONTENTS

St. Valentine's Story

Every February 14, people around the world show their friendship and love for those around them by celebrating Valentine's Day. Valentine's Day has been around for hundreds of years. This holiday, however, has changed greatly since it was first celebrated. The ancient Romans celebrated a Lupercalia, a festival in February in honor of the Roman god **Faunas**. During this holiday, young men and women were paired up in a lottery. Women's names were put in a box, then each young man drew a name from the box. The woman

whose name was drawn became the man's girlfriend for the

next year. The Roman emperor **Claudius II** helped to

start a modern Valentine's Day tradition. In 270 A.D., Claudius passed a law that made marriage illegal. Claudius thought that marriage made men weak and cowardly. One of the early Christian bishops, Valentine, believed strongly in marriage.

He started performing marriages in secret. The emperor had spies who found out what Valentine was doing and arrested him. When Valentine refused to stop performing marriages, Claudius declared that the bishop must die. He sent Valentine to prison, where he would be

In Roman mythology, the woodland god Faunus protected crops, flocks, and shepherds.

The arrest of Bishop Valentine

executed. While Valentine was in prison, he fell in love with a young blind woman who came to visit him. Valentine performed a miracle and gave her back her sight. Before he was taken to be killed, Valentine wrote a note to the young woman. He signed the note "From Your Valentine." Hundreds of years later, people all around the world still use the same message in their valentines. Bishop Valentine was killed on February 14. Because he died a **martyr**, he was made a **saint** by the Catholic Church.

"Valentine" has come to mean "love and affection"

A Day of Honor

More than 200 years later, the Pope decided to end the ancient Roman lottery held each February. Instead, he put the names of Christian saints in the lottery box. Men and women drew the names of saints from the box. For the next year, people had to try to behave like the saints behaved.

After many years, people began to observe this holiday in mid-February as a holy day that celebrated the life of St. Valentine. The modern Valentine's Day grew out of this ancient celebration and church holiday. Valentine's Day

is still considered a special day for people in love and for special friends who wish to share their happy feelings of friendship and devotion.

Mid-February is snowy in many places

The First Valentines

One important Valentine's Day custom is sending cards called valentines. Valentines have been around for many years. In ancient Rome, people looked for marriage partners during mid-winter. Men would send messages to women they wished to date and marry. These cards were sent on February 14. Since this was St. Valentine's Day, these cards came to be called valentines. The oldest existing valentine is in the British Museum in London. It was written in 1415 by the **Duke of Orleans** to his wife. The Duke had been captured in

Unless you say you love me—

I'm goin' out 'n' eat **WORMS!**

the Battle of Agincourt. He was a prisoner in the Tower of

London and wanted his wife to know how much he loved her.

In the 1500s, people began decorating their cards with

Valentines can be funny or sweet

Flowers and hearts appear on many valentines

pictures of Cupid from Roman mythology. Cupid is usually pictured as a smiling, naked baby angel with a bow and arrows. When his arrow hits someone, the person falls in love. Venus, Cupid's mother, is the Roman goddess of love.

Modern Valentines

Over the centuries, valentines have come in many different shapes and sizes. Early valentines were handmade and usually very large and fancy. In the 1800s, books were printed that contained poetry that could be used to help write

Cupid is a messenger of love

valentine messages. In the 1840s, people started buying cards instead of making their own. Esther Howland, a college student, began making valentines to sell to other people. She earned almost $100,000 per year— a fortune in those days! Many valentines are decorated with pictures of different flowers.

Valentines were once written as sonnets, special kinds of poems.

Some people also send flowers on Valentine's Day. Each kind of flower has a meaning attached to it. Roses, for example, are a popular flower to send on Valentine's Day. The red rose is a symbol of pure love. Today, Valentine's Day is a popular

holiday. Millions of people send valentine greetings to their

friends and sweethearts each year—with cards, flowers, and

even boxes of chocolate!

A red rose means "I love you"

Valentine's Day Activity

Giving candy and sweet treats as valentine gifts has become very popular. These foil-wrapped "kisses" are as much fun to make as they are to eat.

What You Need

A freshly mixed bowl of Rice Krispies Treats*
A funnel coated with cooking spray
Waxed paper
A 1-inch by 11-inch (2.5 cm by 28 cm) strip of paper
   for each "kiss"
A 12-inch (30 cm) square of foil for each "kiss"

What You Do

Allow the Rice Krispies Treats* mixture to cool until it's easy to handle. Mold about a cupful (240 ml) inside the funnel. Tip the treat out of the funnel onto the waxed paper. Continue molding "kisses" until all the mixture is used up. Then, label each strip of paper with the words "A Kiss For You!" When the "kisses" are completely cool, wrap each one, along with a paper strip, in foil. Let the strip hang out of the top.

*Trademark of the Kellogg Company

Valentine's Day chocolates

INFORMATION

Index

Words to Know

Claudius II—Roman emperor who persecuted the Christian bishop Valentine and had him executed

Duke of Orleans—a French nobleman who lived in the early 1400s

Faunas—the ancient Roman god of flocks and fields

martyr—a person who dies a courageous death for the love of God and his neighbors

saint—a person given special recognition by the Catholic Church for showing signs of great love and self-sacrifice; martyrs were sometimes sainted

Read More

Bulla, Clyde Robert. *The Story of Valentine's Day*. New York: HarperCollins Publishers, 1999.

Fischer, Sara, and Barbara Klebanow. *American Holidays: Exploring Traditions, Customs, and Backgrounds*. Brattleboro, Vt.: Pro Lingua Associates, 1986.

Kindersley, Anabel. *Celebrations*. New York: DK Publishing, 1997.

Roop, Peter, and Connie Roop. *Let's Celebrate Valentine's Day*. Brookfield, Conn.: The Millbrook Press, 1999.

Internet Sites

Billy Bear's Happy Valentine's Day

http://www.billybear4kids.com/holidays/valentin/fun.htm

Ah Awesome Valentine

http://www.marlo.com/val.htm

Valentine Be Mine

http://techdirect.com/valentine/history.html